# Rebel Grey

# Rebel Grey

## *Poems of Confederate History*

by Zelma Kay Halemeyer

Acclaim Press
MORLEY, MISSOURI

Acclaim Press
— Your Next Great Book —
P.O. Box 238
Morley, MO 63767
(573) 472-9800
www.acclaimpress.com

Publishing Consultant: Duane A. Sikes
Editor: Charles A. Francis
Illustrator: Elizabeth Richter
Book Design: Ron Eifert
Cover Design: M. Frene Melton



Library of Congress Control Number: 2014912658
ISBN-13: 978-1-938905-71-1
ISBN-10: 1-938905-71-7

First Printing: 2014
Printed in the United States of America
10 9 8 7 6 5 4 3 2 1

*This publication was produced using available information.*
*The publisher regrets it cannot assume responsibility for errors or omissions.*

# Contents

# Preface

A ceremony given by the Matthew Fontaine Maury Chapter 1768 of the UDC in honor of their chapter's namesake was to be accompanied by the recitation of a poem. The chosen speaker for the event struggled to find a poem appropriate for the ceremony, thus I wrote *Matthew Fontaine Maury*. This was the first Confederate poem written within this collection. The recitation went beautifully and I was astonished by the interest stirred from this little poem. Thus began a greater project, laden with research and mindful prayer, from which this collection of 36 poems was written.

I would have never endeavored such a task had it not been for the support and encouragement of my loving parents, Linda and Robert and my devoted brother, Dale. I treasure the immeasurable amount of support and warmth from the phenomenal ladies of the Matthew Fontaine Maury Chapter 1768 of the UDC. Especially, I want to give thanks to God who has allowed me to be inspired, and express it in this book.

# Rebel Grey

## *Poems of Confederate History*

# Colonel James Beard at the Battle of Mansfield

These soldiers ceased their battle run
before their fight had really begun
– In hopes of catching a breath of air
their pause meant only death and despair.

This untimely halt in an open field
gave Yankees their target unconcealed
– Lead and doom pounded the men
when Colonel Beard galloped into the din.

Leading his regiment to aid the lone band
he grabbed the colors and into the fray he ran
– A wall of cannon fire and minnies waged fierce
as Beard into its rage he gallantly pierced.

His horse ran swift and bold to the fight
carrying Beard to his last earthly plight
– A musket well aimed struck the brave man
as he fell from his horse his blood swiftly ran.

The Louisiana man lay breathing his last
as his brother to his side quickly rushed
– Pulling James behind a log
his grief spilled over as he panicked and tugged.

Pleading and begging his brother to speak
as James replied not to his longing pleas
– Stillness gripped his lifeless frame
and from his mind fled a tender name.

Twinned upon Beard's lifeless breast
hidden in folds his sentiment confessed
– A pair of baby shoes so small
from the son he left – to fight for – to fall.

Charles, his son was the babe he dreamed of
with hopes and plans of fatherly love
– Picturing his wife and babe safe at home
he died in peace, with the truth unknown.

His wife and son had met the foe
as they were driven from their home
– The helpless babe in homelessness
fell to sleep in heaven's fair rest.

## Poet's Historical Notes:

The Battle of Mansfield was a turning point in Union General Bank's Red River Campaign. Confederate General Richard Taylor seized victory on April 8, 1864 by holding Mansfield and pushing the Yankee invader back. Mansfield was a critical position for the Confederates to hold because if lost, the significant city of Shreveport would become very vulnerable. This was due to the transportation access that the three roads leading out of Mansfield would avail. If lost, Yankee troops would have multiple routes available to surround and seize Shreveport.[1] As the Confederates pushed in victory, Union troops retreated with panic, discarding personal belongings such as canteens, blankets, and rifles.[2]

Colonel James Beard commanded Louisiana's Crescent Regiment and led them bravely in battle. The Crescent Regiment suffered casualties of two hundred from the Battle of Mansfield.[3] Col. Beard died unaware of his family's homelessness and the precious loss of his infant son, of whom he had tiny shoes as a keepsake hidden within his clothes.[4]

1 Mitcham, 143.
2 Winters, 344.
3 Winters, 342.
4 Mitcham, 157-158.

# The Men of Pickett's Charge

Behold! The Immortal Bravery of Men!
These Men Who Marched in Pickett's Division!

Men await under cannon fire
in blazing heat
and bloody mire.
Cannon lead bursting through
Men of Grey
Men of Blue.
Divisions crippled by cannonade
Kemper's casualties
heavily weighed.

Arise! You Fallen of Kemper's Dead!
Take Up Your Arms! Lift Up Your Head!

Aligned to march across the field
Muskets up
the colors wield.
Thundering legion of marching men
faced the foe
faced the din.
Cannons carved the front brigades
muskets strong
against them raged.

Look On! See Garnett Atop His Horse!
Press On You Men! Hold Your Course!

Teeming with their Rebel yell
rushing forward
up the swell.
Eating canister's deadly gall
to take the angle
to take the wall.
Officers joined Death's vast throng
the men alone
their leaders gone.

To the Front, Armistead! Bring Your Men!
You Are the Last of Pickett's Division!

Placing his hat upon his sword
Armistead lead
the valiant forward.
Into the slaughter went the brave
to their death
to their grave.
Strewn across the hallowed land
Thousands of that
noble band.

Where? Cry Out the Ghosts of Grey!
Where, Oh Where, Were the Reserve Brigades?

Alas, but they were not deployed
leaving the engaged
to be destroyed.
Rebs with valor, the Yanks have told
blazed into death
with faces bold.
None have fought as brave as they
These men who spent
their blood of Grey.

Behold! The Noble, Valiant Slain!
Those generals whose illustrious names
of Kemper, Garnett and Armistead
Harken the memory of Pickett's dead.

## Poet's Historical Notes:

On the final day of the Battle of Gettysburg, July 3, 1863 General George Pickett's division was utterly destroyed. Most officers were killed, leaving men with no order or direction. Kemper, Garnett and Armistead were the Brigade commanders, all of which went down. The fighting was fierce and grisly. Losses reported for the brigades are Kemper 60 percent loss, Garnett 65 percent loss, and Armistead 73 percent loss.[1]

Kemper was shot and was informed that his wound was mortal.[2] He miraculously survived his wound but was no longer able to return to the rigors of battle.[3]

Garnett was killed on the battlefield, his insignias were removed from his uniform by souvenir hunters, rendering his remains unidentifiable.[4]

Armistead bravely led his men on foot, leading them with his hat raised high upon his saber.[5] He crossed the wall and was mortally wounded.[6]

General Pickett lost his three brigadier generals in that horrible charge along with all of his field officers except one. Pickett received not a scratch.[7]

The tragedy of the Charge of Pickett's Division is even more heart wrenching with the realization that the officers of the battle were aware of the hopelessness of their charge. Yet their awareness of this error of judgment did not inhibit their obedience and passion in the attack. For duty, honor and their beloved Confederacy they charged into the throng of death.

---

1 Stewart, 264.
2 Stewart, 257.
3 Stewart, 275.
4 Stewart, 250, 275.
5 Commager, 630.
6 Stewart, 216-219.
7 Stewart, 287.

# John S. Mosby Captures General Stoughton

Mixing with the melting snow
Dark and drizzling rain befell
Nighttime narrowed to abyss
Gowning black the moonlight glow
　　Seizing such a night as this
　　Stealing miles of ebony bliss
　　Mosby's Rangers swiftly rode
　　Through the narrow night abyss

Gaining passage through a gap
Cleaved twixt Yankee cavalry lines
Sneaking softly, darkness wrapped
Mosby's men in secret black
　　Entering into enemy lines
　　Deeper and deeper he inclined
　　Mosby's rather devious mind
　　Clever and cunning set the trap

Detailing squads, their duty at hand
Capturing horses and capturing men
Silently, silently without a word
Lest allowing their presence be heard
        One of Mosby's spirited men
        Grabbed the guard of General Stoughton
        Bringing back the prisoner
        Placing him in Mosby's hands

Learning where the officer stayed
(Slumbering sweetly in his bed)
Spurred the men to promptly pay
An imposition of the general's grace
        Upon arrival, Mosby's face
        Gazed upon the peaceful place
        Bounding to the door, he bluntly played
        An awakening for the oblivious
                ...of the Mosby raid

Knocking, knocking till at last
A sleepy staff officer from the window asked
The business of their hammering haste
Deceitfully, Mosby deftly tried
        Professing to be Yankees he plied
        Into the trust of the officer he pried
        The faithful Yank, hurried fast
        Opening the door...he saw the lie

Mosby with a masterful hand
Snatched the scruff of the startled man
Who in his still-warm nightshirt stands
Facing a forceful and daunting leer
　　　　Pulling the prisoner close to hear
　　　　– Muttering "Mosby" into his ear
　　　　Obliging and obeying Mosby's command
　　　　– Leading him to the general's lair

Mosby seeing where the general stayed
– Cozy and comfortable, dreaming away
Covered and clean with soothing peace
Whilst his soldiers in torrents stay
　　　　Stoughton on his stomach lay
　　　　When Mosby whipped back the general's sheets
　　　　Lifting his nightshirt, thus baring Stoughton's seat
　　　　– Mosby slapped General Stoughton awake

Telling him to get to his feet
The waking Stoughton began a scene
Thinking that his officer did take
Too lax a liberty of his place
　　　　Meeting Mosby, he then did see
　　　　His career's detrimental defeat
　　　　Willingly he went with grace
　　　　With Mosby and his men in haste

Escaping through the melting snow
Riding behind Union lines as rain befell
Nighttime narrowed to abyss
Gowning black the moonlight glow
    Seizing such a night as this
    Stealing miles of ebony bliss
    Mosby's Rangers in victory rode
    Through the narrow night abyss

---

Poet's Historical Notes:

John Singleton Mosby rode under General J.E.B. Stuart's command. In the winter of 1863, Mosby gathered a group of cavalrymen to engage and harass the enemy in guerilla warfare.[1] Mosby groomed his men into a tightly disciplined band of fighters, whom could fearlessly undertake the most daring and dangerous endeavors. His purpose in this method of attack was to distract the enemy's focus, and keep the Union resources engaged with trying to find Mosby's Rangers, curbing the Yankee forces from consolidation.[2]

These Confederate guerillas would attack with stealth, stealing horses, information, usable goods and prisoners. Their appearance would come seemingly from nowhere and they would disappear as quickly. This brilliance in planning and the success of their ventures was due to the courage and imagination of the great John Mosby.[3]

---

1 Wert, 31.
2 Wert, 34.
3 Wert, 33.

# One of Grey, One of Blue

brothers meet
in battle's field

one of grey
one of blue

both to kill
both to lose

one from death
one from life

one is laying in heated blood
his battle over
his fight is done

the other with the struggle won
his mortal fight
has just begun

brothers cleaved
in battle's field

        one of grey
        one of blue

                both to kill
                both to lose

the living leaves his mind behind
his heart riven
his aim blind

brothers slain
in battle's field

        one of grey
        one of blue

# J.E.B. Stuart's Raid on General Pope

Stuart with his brilliancy
brought his plan to light
With his flashing cavalry
to put the foe to flight

Quick as lightening
thundering by
Through the raining
August night

Stuart's bold cavalry
neared the sleepy camp
Storming into Yankee dreams
awaking panic's rant

Charging with a rebel yell
scattering Yankees to their flight
Thrilling with their hearts a'swell
full of valiant might

Coursing through the tents
with bursting floods of hope
Alas, they found the tent
belonging to General Pope

Gracing the general's quarters
in happy jubilation
Discovering Pope's papers
exciting Stuart's elation

Quick as lightening
thundering by
Through the raining
August night

Stuart with his cavalry
riding, clothed in victory
Bore the tidings swiftly
to the grateful General Lee

## Poet's Historical Notes:

J.E.B. Stuart's famous raid on General Pope occurred on August 22, 1862 at Catlett's Station, Virginia during the Second Battle of Manassas.[1] The raid proved successful for Stuart's cavalry as they captured more than three hundred prisoners, some of which were Pope's officers. In addition, they confiscated a large sum of money, horses, Pope's military papers, personal property and more. The daring raid boosted Stuart's fame and glory to a new height.[2]

Almost two years later, General Stuart would bravely fight in his last battle.[3] Near Yellow Tavern, Virginia in 1864, Stuart and his men were aggressively trying to hold their ground. As some of the enemy were retreating, a dismounted Yankee cavalryman turned in his flight, aimed and fired his weapon, delivering Stuart a mortal wound.[4]

Stuart's Christian faith gracefully allowed him to accept the closing of his earthly life. He suffered whilst his wound sapped his strength, yet he resigned his will to that of God's will being done. The Confederacy grieved for yet another brilliant officer whose vigor, courage and skill had led and conquered Southern hearts.

1 Dabney, 514-515.
2 McClellan, 94-95.
3 Sorrel, 255.
4 McClellan, 413.

# The Escapades of Madame LaForte and Colonel Zarvona

The beautiful Madame LaForte
Boarded the ship with her manly escort
Her brother she said was he at her arm
Which opened the door for dispensing her charm.

A bounty of trunks she had brought aboard
By kind Union men that fell on her words.
"They're only stock for my new millenary."
She said in broken English a search for to tarry.

The men thought the search would be but a waste
So they carried them to her room with haste
Her promenade with inviting glances
Issued a welcome return of her fancies

The captain himself was entranced by her words
Words that he couldn't believe that he heard.
French phrases of bawdy, saucy flirtations
Guised the Madame's true inclinations

With the captain a fool – like all the rest
For the vixen in that wiggling dress
Madame LaForte's plan ran on track
With only the night to wait for attack

The steamer – *St. Nicholas* kept floating along
Whilst Madame LaForte's men played along.
Docking briefly to board more fares
Amongst newcomers were more men to help set her
lair.

LaForte's men were looking with worry for their
colonel
Not finding the familiar face of Zarvona
At midnight the moment had arrived
For the flirtatious dame to reveal the contrived.

The men of Zarvona discretely were called
To go to the cabin, where LaForte was stalled
Upon their entrance with sheer delight
They saw Zarvona – an amusing sight

He shed the dress and guise of LaForte
And opened the trunks that contained the sport
Of carbines, pistols and swords
With readiness for Zarvona's words

These men that in passenger's guise
With loyalty for the Grey in their eyes
Listened to Colonel Zarvona's instruction
Going at once to bring the Union destruction
The captain aware that his crew was outnumbered
With reasonable reflection he quickly surrendered.

The vessel now in Zarvona's hands
He turned it about to fulfill his plan.

The second phase of his plot began
When early morning he boarded more men
After unloading the passengers Zarvona set out
To capture the USS *Pawnee* – problems started to
mount
With news that the *Pawnee* was far beyond range
With frustration – his plan would change
With every intention of capturing a ship
He turned his focus to a large brig

The *Monticello* would be perfect to catch
Filled with coffee – a valuable snatch
With ease the *St. Nicholas* slid to her side
The men boarded her and became her guide

A crew now set on the *Monticello* took flight
And brought the coffee to Fredricksburg with delight
The majority of Zarvona's men stayed with him
And within the hour they seized another ship again
A schooner called the *Mary Price*
Filled with a cargo of much needed ice.
With another crew of Confederates on board
They carried to Southern hospitals the reward.

Now with the *St. Nicholas'* fuel running low
Zarvona spotted a schooner laden with coal
The *Margaret* they boarded and took control
Filling the *St. Nicholas* up with coal

After the valiant success of his men
A respite in Fredricksburg they would spend
A roaring welcome showered their entry
As they enjoyed the arrival in the fair city

With a beautiful ball given in their honor
Madame LaForte returned in full splendor
A side-splitting shock bestowed on his men
For Zarvona to bring to life once again

That flirty young vixen that smuggled aboard
the weapons that their victory assured
With the rampant laughter flowing
Zarvona played with fun well knowing

His role as the dame in hoop skirts lived on
Enjoying the fun his idea had spun
Years in the future his friends would request
To see once more – their colonel in a dress.

---

Poet's Historical Notes:

Colonel Richard Thomas Zarvona served the Confederacy through his eccentric, adventuresome and brilliant spirit. He was truly unique in many ways. The escapade from which this poem was inspired, was an invention intricately planned by Zarvona. After laying the wild proposal before a board for approval, the feasibility was favorably determined and Zarvona proceeded to attempt his elaborate plan. Happily, he and his men successfully executed the plot, harvesting great rewards for the South.

Colonel Zarvona was later imprisoned, which took a harsh toll on his health and spirit. His sacrifice for the Confederacy lasted longer than just the years at war. Like many soldiers, the after effects of the war left shadows looming through remaining years of life. Zarvona never fully recovered either his health or the spirit that was so brilliant at one time. He died in 1875.

1 http://www.thelatinlibrary.com

# General Lewis Addison Armistead

Man of unflinching valor – racing boldly into death
Raising high his saber – bearing high his hat.

Atop the saber wielding – dancing at the tip
Was the flag of his chapeau – leading his brigade.

Heading the center of Pickett's Charge – storming
fearlessly
Headlong toward the taunting wall – striving victory.

Having reached the destined wall – firing muskets
roared
Stealing life from this brave man – at bloody Gettysburg.

# Belle Boyd

Across the waging
warring lines
Belle with finery sublime
paired with beauty's enrapturing lines
— the enemy engaging
Engaging them with talks of spring
of love and beauty and anything
that pleased the welcoming boy in Blue,
        confiding in her the things he knew

With batting lashes
— flirting eyes
        alluring sighs
— dripping lies
        and lingering sashays
she caught them with their jaw dropped
and reeled them in without a stop
Willingly her catch was caught
        and to the Grey she told the lot

Through the blaze
of shots firing
running ceaselessly untiring
only on herself relying
delivering the news with haste
News that sent the Yankee reeling
for the Southern cause was peeling
loudly from the victory brought
        because of the Yankee without a thought

Occasionally getting caught for spying
she never let her spirits veer
from the Southern cause so dear
her spirits rang out in cheer
Dixie from her throat ringing
Ringing with the zeal of the South
Singing with a heart so proud
As through prison bars she waved
        the beloved flag that flew for the Grey

## Poet's Historical Notes:

The famous heroine of the South, Belle Boyd, proved her patriotism repeatedly through her daring and courageous actions during the war. She risked imprisonment and even death for spying. Eventually, Boyd was placed in the "Old Capitol" prison, which exhausted her health.[1] Even so, she brandished her Rebel spirit in defiance of the Yankees.

Belle led an adventurous life, both during and after the war. She seemed to be a woman whom would not remain idle. Boyd wrote her memoirs, which were published titled *Belle Boyd, In Camp and Prison.* Later she turned to the theatre, becoming an actress and eventually began delivering entertaining dramatic monologues of her adventures during the war.[2]

Boyd was truly a remarkable character, whose active life came to an end in the year 1900, leaving a legacy of Southern spirit and courage to live in America's history.[3]

1 Boyd, 131, 161.

2 Boyd, 9; Sigaud, 187, 195.

3 Sigaud, 200.

# Hold the Line

Prickling, tingling down my spine
when locked the general's eyes to mine
Desperation sealed his solemn gaze
Dissolving my weary muddled haze
Hearing his order, shook my mind
*At all cost* – to hold the line.

Thoughts of my loyal men
Boys with years they'd never spend
Pushed into my tempest brain
Like a demon to unnerve my aim
Seizing control of my mind again
Preparing my men for a fight to the end.

"Boys, the Confederacy is counting on us
This time we *win*. This time we *must*!
No Yank can get past our lines
We are the guard to the flank this time.
We *will* fight!
We *will* prevail!
We are God's soldiers!
We *shall not fail*!
Men! We shall fight to the last of us.
This time we win! This time we must!"

Quickly a shout arose from the men
Exploding a thunder of pride in the din
Contemplating our weaknesses my plan was made
Stationing my ragged, beloved brigade
Anticipation plagued as zeal would wend
Waiting for the wait to end.

At last the noise came to my ear
The clanking, clattering as the enemy neared
My men held their fire as the foe approached
Waiting until within range they encroached
Signaling with a yell ringing clear
"FIRE!" for all my men to hear.

A volley of shots cut through the ranks
Tearing down a wall of the coming Yanks
Shots returned in violent rage
To my fighting, reloading brigade.

Falling to their death in angst
Filling the gaps of the fallen with haste.
Battling, bloodied in comrades mire
Ordering my men to "load and fire"
Until their was no more to load
With bayonets we charged into the fold
Searing steel met the enemy fire
Stabbing, gashing to agony's choir.

Pulverizing flesh with musket butts
Grasping stones to frantically thrust
Fighting as our numbers declined
With thoughts not for the dead behind
The Blue fled in retreat's hurried gust
As gore strewn across the settling dust.

Perspiration trickled down my spine
As Victory failed to make us blind
The fallen, a carpet of crimson sheen
As the moans and cries surpassed all we'd seen
Burning, fusing into my mind
The bitter cost – to hold the line.

# Weevils in my Vittles

Gnawing in my haversack
are weevils in my hardtack.
I could swear I hear them as we march
Louder and louder they chomp and munch.

Looking at my destined meal
makes my stomach sickly reel.
If only my hunger would deplete
(as my palate longs for something to eat).

Gazing at my meal awriggle
a haven for bugs are my vittles
Worms that wiggle in bold delight
never shirking at my sight.

Closing my eyes and taking a bite
swallowing with relief and delight
That those worms that wiggled so
ceased their jiggle when below.

Those critters...how they baffle me
gets me how they came to be
living in my hardtack
gnawing in my haversack.

# Raphael Semmes and the *Alabama*

Gasping for the salt sea air
Pining pounding waves beneath
Yearning for the breakers breaking
Spraying salty sea to taste.

Sailing for the waiting waters
Cunning Captain Semmes set out
Applying keen his wit and wisdom
Fighting fervently for the South.

Sailing his ship — sleek and sliding
Gliding, groping dark waves shining
Plowing sea in floating furrows
Hunting hungrily for the foe.

Pursuing enemies valued vessels
Trapping trading ships of wealth
Inflicting wounds from supply striking
Crippling commerce with clever stealth.

Sending shot o'erhead with warning
Quelling quickly the foe to cease
Grappling close in busy boarding
Swiftly seizing the prized feast.

Striking terror in watery wake
Pirating pigeons for the Grey's sake
Strangling pockets of the fattened Fed
Destroying, demoralizing Yankee trade.

Retiring at last to restore and repair
Leaking lips reaching the enemy ear
Sending an enemy pointedly pouncing
Lurking, lingering in the harbor near.

Gleaming *Kearsarge* was the warship
Hovering, hankering for the attack

Trapping Semmes into waging war
Leasing lead in full offence
Damaging not the capable *Kearsarge*
Receiving her roaring, well aimed blasts.

Exploding bursts of shrapnel shouting
Shearing sheets and masts of wood
Smoking clouds of sulpher stinking
Blazing blasts whizzing through.

Sinking ship was the awed *Alabama*
Abandoning after so many years
Diving to the waiting waters
Sinking slowly in salty tears.

Swimming, floating in watery wake
Slipping Semmes his leave did take
Escaping capture with many men
Eluding the enemy once again.

Thinking of his home afar
Sailing slowly thoughts run swift
Stinging pictures of love left
Longing lonely family dear.

Gasping for the clear cool air
Pining peace beneath his feet
Yearning for the greenery growing
Splashing sweet perfumes to taste.

## Poet's Historical Notes:

Raphael Semmes traveled extensively over the seas as captain of the *Alabama.* Semmes finally reunited with his wife after an absence of three years and nine months. The detachment from his family during these war years at sea was difficult, especially since correspondence was impeded by the intrusion of war.[1]

The *Alabama* was built to be a sleek and swift raider. She was armed and fitted for coal and sail so she could be independent for long sea voyages. She was a fast predator as well as a quickly escaping quarry, whichever scenario arrived her speed was her boon.[2] Semmes' experience gave him the grace to handle her well for her time serving the Confederacy. Semmes and the*Alabama*'s exploits were splashed over newspapers and dime novels much to the entertainment of both the North and South.[3]

This hero of the Confederacy served well, in crippling the Yankees where they would bleed most – economically. His plan was to prevent commerce, which would disrupt the Union's everyday life. Whilst the South was being invaded and their lives turned upside down, the Yankees were still going to the opera, parties, etc. The citizens had not felt the war until Semmes' raid on the import/export business of the Union. Thus, Semmes did more for the Confederacy in hurting the Yankee morale, as well as distracting the Union blockade in their exhaustive hunt for the elusive *Alabama.*[4]

1 Fox, 236.
2 Fox, 7.
3 Fox, 171-174.
4 Fox, 88.

# The Picket's Truce

Peaceful and Pure
winter's pearls
circled the darkened ground

Floating, Falling
spreading peace
quieting every sound

Serene and Soft
a blanket of white
spread like angel's wings

Lulling lowly
the stop of time
creating a heavenly scene

Calm and Cool
the moonlit night
thawed the clouded soul

Gently...Gently
a Southern song
serenaded from the foe

Coaxing, Carrying
a happy tear
inviting a Yankee tune

Fond and Friendly
the Rebs replied
with the nation's anthem

Tarrying, trading
coffee and tobacco
praying for lasting peace

Secretly Stealing
a moment in time
with the picket's truce

Poet's Historical Notes:

Truly, during war a soldier's life is wracked with the most intense and most boring sensations. Not uncommon during the war did an unspoken truce take place between opposite pickets. Boredom and human curiosity played a role with these little truces. It brought a personal element of understanding across the lines of war. They would trade this for that, maybe a coat for meat or coffee for tobacco, in their own way, their exchange was a breaking of the bread with a fellow soldier.[1]

1 Davis, 220; Wilkinson and Woodworth, 111.

## Joanna Fox Waddill

To the bloody battle lines
going headstrong to the gore
Owning will of her own mind
her youth to be no more
Duty to the Grey did bind
her heart forevermore.

The stench of blood filled the air
through the lagging days
Haggard men once young and fair
aged early into grey
With dedicated constant care
she nursed the price they paid.

Never shirking from demand
from Confederates she held dear
Roving o'er the bleeding land
the fighting she stayed near
Enduring service from her hand
and heart she gave for years.

Rescuing the flag so dear
    on that fateful day
When the enemy force came near
    she bore the flag away
Hiding it from capture feared
    within her skirts it stayed.

To the bloody battle lines
    going headstrong to the gore
Owning will of her own mind
    memories now she bore
Of nursing those her heart did bind
    their faces evermore.

---

Poet's Historical Notes:

Joanna Fox Waddill was one of many brave women whom served in the war as a nurse. Waddill traveled throughout the war, going to the battle lines to serve Confederate wounded. Hospitals were a horrific sight when filled with the wounded. Treatment was often amputation, which was commonly followed by gangrene, which likely would result in death. The screams of men during operations without sedation would sicken the strongest of constitutions, permeating memories throughout a lifetime. Joanna Waddill's constancy as a frontline nurse is a true witness to her determination and courage.

# Battle of the Crater

The spark of morning lit the dawn
rousing Confederate men
whilst Union troops' plan of hell
opened that fateful morn

Having prepared for this day
the black Union troops were trained
But fearing political repercussions
at the last – the troops were changed.

Their leaders not making aware
the men now substituting
of the path that they should take
at the sounding blare

This expected signal din
would come from their labored mine
which packed up tight with gunpowder
lay 'neath the Confederate men.

The rumbling dragon in all its fury
spewed the shaking earth
engulfing men with fiery sod
to horribly and viciously bury

A massive crater from the blast
carved Confederate terrain
To pluck the maimed Confederate troops
the Yankees advanced in haste.

Into the crater the Union gushed
wrongly deeming it safe
Finding instead the trap they set
upon themselves had crushed

The diabolical Union plan
had recoiled itself on them
like a beast unleashed
its lead not held by man

Confederates decked the rim
of the pit that held their quarry
firing without requiring aim
at the Yanks below within

The Yanks fell in numbers fast
as they tried to find escape
losing the battle that they had waged
with that wretched earthen blast.

The carnage of that sorry day
etched in the minds of men
tangling misery in memory
of the hell they had to pay.

## Poet's Historical Notes:

General Ambrose Burnside was the Union officer who gave the approval for the plans of the mine. The tunneling began June 25 and was finished on July 23, after which it was packed with explosives.[1] On the early morning of July 30, 1864 a massive explosion erupted, sending flames of earth, with men and lumber heavenward.[2]

The division that Burnside had chosen to mount the attack that day was Ferrero's division of black troops. Burnside had briefed Ferrero of the plan, so Ferrero's troops were drilled accordingly, making them supremely alert, and prepared for action. However, General's Meade and Grant nixed Burnside's big plan of using Ferrero's black troops, for political reasons. Their thoughts pondered on what people would think sending black men first into battle to be killed. Hence, unprepared troops were substituted and failed miserably.[3] If the original plan of engaging Ferrero's troops had been used, the results would have likely favored the Union.

1 Commager, 1018.
2 Garrison, 262-263.
3 Garrison, 261.

# Jefferson Davis

An inherited pride of America's freedom
Coursed the veins of the Davis' home
Equipping young Jeff with the tool of knowledge
A sacred gift, tendered by his parentage

With military schooling, he grew to a man
Fighting in the Mexican war, serving his countrymen
Carrying courage with a cool command
Leading unfalteringly, with a firm, skilled hand

Entering politics and studying law
In Jefferson Davis, the people saw
A charming man, distinguished and elegant
With a persuasive and captivating intellect

This dignified and dedicated orator
Stood firm on principles of the founding fathers
With rights bestowed in the Constitution
The Union provoked its own dissolution

Jefferson Davis with the pride of the South
Conceded to give the gifts of his mouth
As speaker and defender of the cause
Repelling tyranny from enslaving with laws

Elected by the Confederacy
Jefferson Davis humbly took the presidency
Applying his experience with thoughtful deliberation
Making fateful decisions for his beloved nation

The burden of responsibility
Weighing on his shoulders heavily
Bearing the blood of victory and defeat
Carrying hope, when hope was depleting

The close of the war brought misery
To the South and the Davis family
Seized with tyrannical treachery
Davis imprisoned without legality

Spending years in incarceration
Allowed Davis biblical meditation
Developing a closer relationship in Christ
Finally receiving inner peace at last

This peace instilled within his breast
Quelled the fight, he put to rest
Seeking now his family united
Which the war had torn and the enemy spited

Plagued with problems of family now scattered
And health declining and financial matters
He showed his grit in facing his trials
Regretting never the fight for the cause

For honor and duty, he served with pride
His personal wants and comforts he set aside
Believing his principles to be just and true
Unto his death for these rights he pursued

## Poet's Historical Notes:

Jefferson Davis became the elected president of the Confederacy in 1861.[1] As with any significant leader, judgments of his actions have been substantial. However, one thing is indisputable about Davis, and that is his adherence to his principles throughout his lifetime. He did not vary from his course during times of peace, war or imprisonment.[2]

Like many of the war's officers, he was a graduate of West Point.[3] His exemplary education had great bearing on his future of war and politics, allowing him to become a gifted speaker and a persuasive leader inspiring to the people. After the war, his finances were a disaster and he never regained the wealth he had prior to the war. Yet through the life altering war, and all the implications of change, he kept alive a brilliant hope for the nation.[4]

1 Cooper, 328.
2 Cooper, 658.
3 Cooper, 40.
4 Cooper, 635.

# The Sacrifice

I never felt the bullet hit
Realization struck at the sight of it
Flowing as a beautiful spring
Crimson with my life draining.

The battle noise seemed far away
like from another world and another day
A coolness gripped my sweaty frame
serene and quiet a darkness came
followed by a welcoming swell
of voices sweet and joyous church bells

At last a light opened my eyes
I saw at once in glorious surprise
the ones I loved and had missed for years
now at my welcome, sang melodious cheers

The most important peace did I see,
was the One who bled and died for me
Happy was He at my journey's end
and that I gave my life for a friend.

His love encircled me with a warmth so full
Complete peace and joy filled my cleansed soul.

---

*"Greater love has no one but this,
than to lay down one's life for his friends."*
—John 15:13, NKJV

# Captain Doc Rayburn Meets Limber Jim

Masquerading as a belle
Doc donned a ballroom dress
His blue eyes and slight young frame
And his flaxen tresses
Got him to a Yankee ball
Where he whirled and danced
Swishing his skirts around the room
He listened to their plans
Then taking leave of the dance
He spied a fine black beast
An officer's mount it was
That lonely horse teased

Chuckling to himself, he sauntered
Over to the mount
Swinging his leg over the saddle
His skirts billowed about
Flowing as he rode along
Quickly making way
Taking with him as he left
The plans he heard them say
Returning to his camp with glory
His raiders greeted him
With slaps of praise and laughter
They met his horse – named Limber Jim.

# Patrick Cleburne at Ringgold Gap

Cleburne resilient, faced the odds
Outnumbered – he fought, regardless of cost.
Ensured that his division was on its own
The burden lay on his shoulders alone.

His mission to hold Hooker's forces back
By guarding the gorge known as Ringgold Gap.

With Hooker hugging close the Confederate heels
Cleburne's nerve stayed cool as steel.
Crafting quick a devious trap
He carefully positioned his men for attack.

Screened within the pass' entry
Cleburne placed some heavy artillery.
Backing them with infantry support
Flooding the gap with Confederate force.

Perched on opposite sides of the ravine
The flanking positions lay sight unseen.
The Confederates poised and ready to fight
Laying still and silent, hidden from sight.

Anxiously awaiting as nerves prickled keen
Watching the Yanks march into the scene.
Steady thundering of the marching feet
Echoed the eager Confederate heartbeat.

The Union troops were a sea of blue
Nearing the gap, they split in two.
One arm flanked and the other went in
Nearing the Confederate artillery poised within.

Cleburne remained cool and steady
Watching the approach of the massive enemy.
Closer they came until at last
Cleburne signaled to fire the artillery blast.

The artillery men rushed quick to remove
the shrubs and brush that had hid them from view.
The roar of the cannon bore into the men
leveling the Union – they fired again.

The flanking position was held at bay
As Hooker's troops stormed to the fray.
Cleburne reinforced those men on his flank
Pushing back the failing, fighting Yank.

Hours and hours of Union persistence
Claimed casualties of Yankees by hundreds.
Finally feeling they hadn't a chance
Allayed attack instead of advance.

Hindering Hooker's plan for victory
Cost Cleburne's men a loss of twenty.
With winning resolve, when his mission was through
Honorably he and his men withdrew.

Standing solid at Ringgold Gap
Bravely bearing the brunt of attack.
Inspiring his men with unyielding zest
By their side, fought the Stonewall of the West.

## Poet's Historical Notes:

On a late November morning of 1863, the Battle of Ringgold Gap began.[1] Major General Patrick Cleburne had been ordered by General Braxton Bragg to guard and hold the gap to delay the Union advance on the Confederate retreat.[2] Bragg had not given any advisement on how this gargantuan feat was to be executed, leaving Cleburne to his own devises.[3] Cleburne was greatly aware that he would be enormously outnumbered and that his tactical plan would be critical to their success. His forethought and vision made him one of the best combat tacticians during the war.[4] Superbly did he position and lead his troops on the field of battle. His plan was magnificently unfurled in victory as his men held back the goliath of Hooker's men from surmounting Ringgold Gap.[5] About a year after this battle, the Confederacy would lose this exceptional leader in the Battle of Franklin.[6]

1 Symonds, 173.
2 Joslyn, 116.
3 Joslyn, 119.
4 Brown, 238.
5 Symonds, 175.
6 Joslyn, 277-279.

# The Grey and the Red

left at peace to live at will
enjoying scents of sweet honeysuckle
blooms of white on sleepy trees
draped in southern waking dreams

luscious green bathed in dew
tears of morning awake camellia blooms
thundering soldiers of blue storm in
raging the peaceful life to end

just as with the men of red
spoiling the soil, with the stubborn dead
unwilling to relinquish to foreign ways
to hold to their land, in death would stay

clinging to the vast blue skies
holding the eagle in honored eyes
trees and creatures of talking life
whispering of the coming strife

the grey and the red would fight and die
losing the old way of life
the towering giant of blue would see
once more their quest to kill beauty

echoes of the past still live
in noble hearts whose blood still gives
the yearning remembrance of freedom's demise
when looking at the blue, blue skies

Poet's Historical Notes:

During the war between the North and the South, there was also an ongoing war between the United States and some tribes of North American Indian peoples. This history that took place coinciding with the time of the War Between the States, sometimes is overlooked. Both the North American Indian and the Southerner suffered invasion by the Union, which determined to impose its way of life upon the opposition. In both cases, the aggression of the enemy prevailed and forever changed a way of life for the North American Indian and the Southerner.

# Nancy Hart

With hatred inside that grew
At the discovery of her kin they slew
The Union her determination
To smite with utter obliteration

Experienced well with guns and the wild
Her beauty an attribute to the Union beguiled
Allowing her to slip in and out
The Union lines to mill about
Attentively listening to their chatter
Honing in on the subjects that mattered
Taking with her all that was plied
She returned to the Confederates for whom she had spied.

The backwoods life that she had lived
Gave her another contribution to give
Knowing well the land and terrain
A position as scout and guide she retained.
The acquired skills she had with a gun
Were assumed non-existent of the fair woman
By the Union who had captured young Nancy
Locking her up – one man took a fancy
To the young lass with dark flowing hair
For freedom, she would anything dare

Confronting Miss Hart with his flirtation
She seized his gun without hesitation
And aiming the gun with stealth to his head
Pulling the trigger... at once...he was dead.

The rundown house that had been her jail
Now through its open window she sailed
A jumble of tall weeds cushioned her fall
With the two-story drop, she had no time to stall

The Yankees would be close on her heels
So the first horse she saw — was the one she would steal
Riding the mount barebacked through the night
Pushing her way past Union sight
Returning to her family of defenders
She continued to fight the war that was hers
And every one that loved their home
That saw the ruin that stood alone
Abandoned by all that was green and growing
Now dead and hollow — with no life bestowing
The ones that were loved now gone to their grave
Only freedom for the living - To fight for - To save.

## Poet's Historical Notes:

Nancy Hart was living a rustic backwoods lifestyle, through which she had acquired an essential knowledge of her surroundings. She was exceptional at shooting and riding as well. These traits gave the Confederacy a seasoned scout and guide. In addition, her beauty and youth allowed her to be an effective spy.

Nancy was a strong-willed young woman who joined the Moccasin Rangers, a group of guerrilla fighters. She did not shirk her devotion to the South, but fought for it in any and every way she could. Her deeds were numerous. Her determination was sure. Boldness and courage proudly endeared her to her people as a Southerner, a Confederate, a Patriot and a Rebel.

# Matthew Fontaine Maury

through loyal reading of the Word
he understood words before unheard
Psalm 8 echoed in his mind persistently
the paths of the sea, the paths of the sea.

a pursuit to benefit all mankind
through searching logbooks he would find
records of currents, winds and calm
patterns depicting paths marked in Psalm.

Ecclesiastes 1 verse 6 tells of the wind
concealed on pages, revealed to him
laws of perpetual whirling he finds
to always return the same course in time.

recording his findings – maps he would write
baring the secrets the sea held from sight.
the Northwest Passage he surmised
through research divined the disguised

for beloved Virginia he joined the war
he served his home from near and far
through weaponry and purchasing ships
diplomat carrying peace on his lips.

constant companion to him was the sea
whether on land or water he be
to him was a passion from early youth
always to sea -- to seek the truth.

through taking the Scriptures literally
he taught us what faith should be
the Word Is... and says what shall be.
the paths of the sea, the paths of the sea.

## Poet's Historical Notes:

Matthew Fontaine Maury joined the United States Navy when he was nineteen, gleaning from his time at sea the excitement and wonderment of the world.[1] After an accident rendered him unfit for sea duty, he served the U.S.N. through his research.

Maury's quest for knowledge led him to become the father of oceanography. His inquisitive mind untangled the mysteries of the sea, enabling him to chart currents and winds.[2] This magnificent effort allowed seamen to follow Maury's charts which outlined a safer and quicker route to travel. This affected sea travel internationally, improving navigational sailing entirely.[3] Maury's vast accomplishments in science coupled with his thorough knowledge of the Bible, on which he found sound basis for laws and principles of understanding the motions of wind and currents.

Maury wrote of his discoveries, having many of his works published, one of which, *The Physical Geography of the Sea*, became a highly respected work of science, which is remarkably understandable to the laymen. Seamen that read and followed Maury's advice and principles of understanding patterns of the sea and winds fared better at sea than those that did not. His development of the research that he accumulated formed a basis for oceanography and metrological sciences.[4]

When the War Between the States erupted, Maury, a native Virginian, resigned from the U.S.N. and gave his service to Virginia.[5] Maury's achievements developed further as he was appointed "Chief of the Sea-Coast, Harbor, and River Defenses of the South."[6] Rather than his usual pursuits in science, he turned his efforts to the further development of the torpedo.[7]

Maury's pursuits in science continued throughout his life, becoming internationally recognized and respected.[8] His dedication gave the world the gifts of his genius as he shared his findings openly to benefit all mankind.

---

1 Corbin, 14.
2 Hearn, 113-114.
3 Hearn,121, 124.
4 Hearn, 195.
5 Hearn, 223.
6 Corbin, 198.
7 Corbin, 199.
8 Hearn, 189.

# Bittersweet

Through her anguish swelled salty tears
from defeat of stolen tender years
Yet her face would once again shine sweet
In a peace, so bittersweet.

Bittersweet for the cause now lost
For the sons the war had cost
For the sons that peace would spare
Mingling joy with despair.

Her children's blood had stained her dress
Of fields and valleys now at rest
Time would wash the blood away
Leaving in her heart the stain.

The South in graceful pride coaxed
The beauty that only she can boast
Mending and primping her exquisite form
Springing new life, in radiance born.

Memories of the days gone by
Of the cause for which her sons died
Patched with stones, the battlefields seen
Gowned in splendor in luscious green.

Reminiscence of her boys in Grey
Which through her splendor no more would play
Gone were they, in heaven to meet
Bringing a peace, so bittersweet.

# CSS *Virginia*

Rising from the river water, the slope-roofed
ironclad moved north
a smoke stream billowed from the stack
perched on the frigate's roof
With bold attempt to carve a dent
into the enemy battery,
the *Virginia* headed to Newport News
to stagger the Union mentality.

The *Virginia* with intent for utter destruction
was shielded by 4 inch iron plating
and armed with an iron prow
below the bow waters waiting
Guns abroad, stem and astern
to always the enemy face
and a commander of experience to coax
from the awkward tub a dance of grace.

She glided her way through
 the calm and quiet waters
Sighting the enemy multitude
 *Virginia* held her course
Amongst over a dozen federal vessels
 no one spied their demise approaching
Until at last the *Congress* fired a round
 toward the *Virginia* encroaching
among the host of vulnerable craft
 lazy with months of rest
The *Virginia* now receiving shot
 from the startled gunboats pressed
straight into the rain of lead
 her guns in silence loomed
waiting for the moment when her aim and fire
 would strike a mortal wound.

CRASH! – The *Virginia* let loose a shot
 from her bow rifle a tremendous blast.

Tearing a hole in the *Cumberland*
 The *Virginia*'s deadly lead passed
And with a chance to finish the crippled sloop of war
 the *Virginia* with determined aim
rammed the 6 foot prow into the hull
 of the *Cumberland* mortally maimed.

Meanwhile, the *Virginia* received assault
from the frigate, USS *Congress*
Swatting her with broadsides and guns well aimed
the *Virginia* did her best
Driving the *Congress,* beaten and scared
to retreat from the battle scene
her sails hell bent to run for shore
with a plan they thought was keen.
Intending the *Congress* to run aground
striking her colors, she raised
— the flag of white
— a surrendering sight
— to all who upon it gazed.
Immediately the firing stopped
and a Confederate gunboat made way
as the *Congress* raised a second white flag
the surrender well conveyed.

The Confederate gunboat, in good faith
approached the *Congress*' side
along the starboard the gunboat glided
and the *Congress* revealed her lie
Blazing their guns at the Confederates
whilst under the flag of white
The *Congress* paired with men ashore
pummeled them with pure delight

The Confederate gunboat now caught in crossfire
shaken tried to leave
as the *Virginia* waited with abomination
for revenge impatiently seethed
Now the gunboat *Raleigh*'s decks
were littered with bloodied and war torn men
whom had sheathed the sword of battle
with a peaceful hand to lend
With the *Raleigh* clear, the *Virginia*
pounded the Union on shore
The *Congress* in flames of retribution
a blazing inferno wore

The Union trembled at
the *Virginia*'s invincible nature
their only chance to curb destruction
was to bring forth the *Monitor*
– A boxlike ironclad
with a shorter draft
Making it the more
maneuverable of the dueling ironclads.

The *Virginia* on the following morn
set out to resume the battle
when upon a hump they had run aground
becoming completely immobile
Spying a flat, boxlike craft
directing its course straight
– to the *Virginia* to bring the battle
without a moment to wait

The *Virginia,* stuck upon the Middle Ground
of Hampton Roads, struggled to break free
knowing the craft approaching fast
as the *Monitor* they could clearly see
Powerfully opening fire as soon
as the *Monitor* was in range
She cast hundred pounders at the *Virginia*
who returned the same

Finally the *Virginia* broke free
from the confounded mass of ground
allowing freedom of motion
to turn the tables around
Matched opponents beat the sides
of each others ship without
a mortal shot for either craft
only will to endure would win out

Ramming the *Monitor* repeatedly
        and hailing upon her lead
The *Monitor* retreated to the shoal
        with haste from the *Virginia* fled
Knowing the draft of the *Virginia*
        kept her from following
the *Monitor* lay in retreat
        with ne'er a sign of going
The *Virginia* with anticipation
        of the battle yet to prove
waited as time ticked by – slowly by
        for the enemy to make her move
An hour of time was enough to wait
        for an enemy too scared to fight
Leaving the scene, the *Virginia*
        in her iron fist clutched tight
– a victory of a battle
        – won hard and rough
                – with honor and with might.

## Poet's Historical Notes:

The battle between the *Monitor* and the *Merrimack,* as it is so often called, was actually the battle between the *Monitor* and the CSS *Virginia.* The *Merrimack* had been rebuilt into the CSS *Virginia,* hence the confusion. In addition, the result of the battle has often been told and retold as being a stalemate. However, at the time of the battle it was perceived that the Confederates had won, since the *Monitor* had disengaged for so long. Oftentimes the true history of an event is clouded by the account repeated by the victor.

# The Orphan Brigade

Kentucky's fair melodious sons
left her Bluegrass feathered hills
to lift her freedom above all else.

South, they'd go
to lands unknown
pocketing dreams of their home.

Kentucky spirit amassed the brave
of the Bluegrass' fighting Grey
forming the First Kentucky Brigade.

South, they'd remain
as their homeland
lay grasped within the enemy hand.

Union Kentucky despised her Rebel sons
severing all ties and word from home
abandoning these men, now orphans alone.

Forging on
Kentucky's sons
faced the enemy's hammering guns.

Bleeding, dieing – with inextinguishable light
bringing the enemy a menacing fight
tenaciously battling with a matchless might.

O'er the lands
these bleeding ones
flowed Kentucky's finest sons.

Kentucky birthed this valiant breed
born with pride, sewn with grit
heady with determined spirit.

Together they banded
Together they made
The Kentucky First, known as the Orphan Brigade.

## Poet's Historical Notes:

Kentucky was vied for by both the Union and Confederacy. Her position of neutrality only split her citizens in fighting a war literally brother against brother. Kentucky ultimately was declared a Union state.[1] This made furloughs impossible for the Confederate Kentuckians, and it also left the state's mail in Union hands, so delivery of mail was complicated and unreliable.[2] Contrary to what would be expected morale under such circumstances, they were renown for their cheerful spirit which seemed to prevail within the brigade.[3] This vigorous band of determined men were the best of the best. They were in the most heated battles and fought heroically, suffering more casualties than any other by comparison throughout the war.[4] In spite of this also, their desertion rates were unusually low.[5] They were truly a remarkable breed of men, whom despite their ultimate loss, they did not fall to despair, but kept fighting the fight of hope.

1 Brown, 277.
2 Davis, 138.
3 Davis, 245.
4 Brown, 298.
5 Brown, 294.

# The Bullet in the Book

Through the flesh of pierced pages
Parting the conquering print of ages
Ceasing death by a jolting grasp
Seizing lead in a clench steadfast.

Into the tattered pocket he reached
Retrieving the object the bullet had breached
Locking his eyes in astonishment
To the bondage of the bullet spent.

Crimson blanched to shocking pallor
Beholding the book with blooming ardor
Flushed he felt a baptismal flood
For this that saved his very blood.

Opening the cover with life anew
Seeing in faith, hope in view
Perusing through the unturned pages
Feeding on the Promise of ages.

At last into the Word he would look
Because of the bullet in the book.

## Poet's Historical Notes:

Carried in many pockets during the war was a small Bible. Different people naturally had different reasons for carrying it. Some were quite religious and made a practice of regularly studying the Word. This poem is about the other folks, the ones that have the Word readily available, and yet have not felt the need or urgency to call on God. A brush with death sometimes awakens urgency within a lost or wandering soul.

# Doc Rayburn and his Phantom Unit

Antsy for some wartime action
Doc talked up his plan
To a flock of eager youths
He aimed to make his band

> 'Adventures beyond your wildest dreams
> Far away from home
> Kicking the Union in the seams
> Will be our only goal
> Fighting for our independence
> With all we have to give
> Striking at the Union
> So we can freely live.'

Eagerly the fighting youths
Joined with Rayburn's plan
Doing everything they could
To smite the Yankee hand

Electing Doc their captain
he led the eager fold
on rampage of the Union camps
with vigor quick and bold

Through action both swift and sly
by these guerillas so tightly knit
Inspired a fear through Union troops
of this group they called...the Phantom Unit.

---

Poet's Historical Notes:

Howell "Doc" Rayburn enlisted in the Texas cavalry and at sometime he became either sick or wounded, at which point, he was left behind at a hospital to recover. During this time of recuperation, he persuaded a bunch of youths to join him and he created a small company that engaged in guerilla warfare, which terrified the Union. This Phantom Unit was recognized by the Confederate Army and eventually served with General Sterling Price during the Missouri Campaign of 1864.[1]

"Doc" was such a detriment to the Union that they placed a reward on his head. Late in the war, he was captured and spent time in prison. Rayburn's physical health was weak and combined with poor treatment in prison, resulted in his contraction of tuberculosis. He died shortly thereafter, when he was yet in his mere 20s.[2]

1 www.rootsweb

2 www.rootsweb

# Turner Ashby

Both daring and noble
modest and humble
Carrying a Christian heart
of exuberant vitality
This gallant gentleman
and master horseman
of fair Virginia's best
The valiant, Turner Ashby

From his careful lips
words chosen clean and crisp
pure for any lady's ear
hearkened his high morality
Likened to his honorable language
his deeds were equally engaged
Ever mindful of his manners
The chivalrous, Turner Ashby

With the hammer
of war's clamor
Ashby flew to serve
with loyalty and love to guide
Born to be a leader
going headlong into danger
Taking with him willing men
full of Southern pride

The callous murder
of his brother
kindled a furious fire
Vowing to vanquish the murderous foe
his mourning breast
would take no rest
With a vigilant, perceptive eye
ever for the fight aglow

Fearlessly attacking
with his numbers sorely lacking
fighting with a terrible might
despite all personal injury
Blazing forth into the flesh
the frightened enemy's mind would mesh
their horror and their terror
with the name of Turner Ashby.

## Poet's Historical Notes:

Brigadier General Turner Ashby was an accomplished horseman who heroically commanded Stonewall Jackson's cavalry in the Army of the Valley. Ashby lacked discipline within his cavalry and yet he capably led his men through inspiration, passion and bravery.[1] His fierce aggression in battle invigorated the blood of his men to the same determination. His men gave a magnificent shout of "Ashby" racing into battle's thrall, inciting the Yankees to fear from the well known and dreaded name of Turner Ashby.[2]

1 Dabney, 327.

2 Dabney, 261.

# Freedom's Fight

Used until their coffers filled
Took advantage of Southern good will
Striking with the iron hot
The Union concealed their calculated plot
Whilst teaming the media to their political agenda
And feeding the ignorant with their propaganda
The Union delayed with trickery and deceit
In order to arm and position their soldiers for the
blood feast.

Taxing the South and impressing rules
The federals employed all its forceful tools
Badgering the South to relinquish her rights
The sovereign states with independent might
Resisted the threats and provocation
Wanting no blood shed in this great nation

Dictating child was the Union's position
To the sovereign states, the parent of its union
With disgust from torment so bold
Arose the dissension against federal rule
Such was the gluttony of power in the Union
Railing against its Constitution
The South without desire for war
Bided her time, till time was no more

Lincoln without congressional authority
Declared war on April 15th
Upon South Carolina and the Confederacy
And gathered a force to invade the South without pity
The federals, with the first aggression of war
Sported to see Southern blood poured

Newspapers reported with scathing lies
Gaining support for the federal lines
Inciting rash hatred for Southerners
From Northern pulpits, meetings and papers

With the political die now thrown
Inciting a war to smother her own
Citizens and patriots whom had loved
Their United States, which now had shoved
The burden of war upon the South's lands
Defending herself from her own countrymen

A fight for the rights of sovereignty
Against the evils of tyranny
Was the simple cause so pure
That many would fight and endure
A forever threat to this, our Union
Is the ignorance which thieves – to subjugate our
  Constitution.
– Fight as those whom fearlessly died
From tyrants that lure the public with political lies.
Fight with Knowledge, for Freedom, for which so many
  have died.

# Emma Sansom meets General Forrest

the gentle hand
of a tender man
reached down from upon his horse
easing young Emma upon his steed
and setting upon their course

the youthful guide
upon their ride
revealed the path to take
showing him to the ford
for Confederacy's sake

the placid creek
whispering sweet
warned of danger awaiting
the gentle man, bid Emma stay
easing down the young lady

the single track
echoed back
as Forrest perused the scene
throwing his glance behind, he spied
the following youthful teen

the spunky maid
by him stayed
to help if trouble arose
determined to stand at Forrest's side
courage bloomed in this Confederate rose

the silence broke
as muskets spoke
the Union's presence declared
Emma waved her feminine bonnet
proudly in the air

the violence ceased
as a human peace
graced the hearts of men
Blue and Grey, blurred as one
in awe of the brave young Emma

## Poet's Historical Notes:

In dogged pursuit of Union Colonel Streight and his troops, General Forrest had stayed consistently close to the retreating enemy. However, Streight's troops managed to cross the bridge over the Black Warrior River and burn the bridge after them, hoping to squelch Forrest's pursuit. General Forrest went to a nearby farmstead and queried for directions to an alternate crossing of the river. Emma Sansom was the young lady whom ran to his assistance and volunteered to show the way.[1] Upon reaching the crossing, she bravely withstood enemy fire as she defiantly waved her bonnet in the air.[2] Ultimately, Sansom's eagerness to help the Confederate General allowed him to succeed in capturing the retreating Colonel Streight.[3]

1 Davidson and Foxx, 148.

2 Davidson and Foxx, 149.

3 Henry, 291.

# Robert E. Lee

The general upon Traveller rode
        As pressing tears stung his eyes
Trodding at a steady pace
        Knowing his dream had died

Through the veil of salty pools
        His eyes beheld a blur
Of men aglow with love for him
        – his soldiers who loyally served

Silence stole across the crowd
        As their gaze embraced the sight
Of Lee so grieved and sorrowful
        for the cause he deemed as right

His tender heart broken in two
        Left an empty void
Pain...anguish and despair
        for the hope destroyed

Duty...love and respect
Of his brave, worn men
Inspired Lee to speak
Addressing them once again

Tortured with the aching knot
Tight with sorrows pain
Forcing his voice to speak
His composure he forced to maintain

His last words dripped with heart
Full...clear and true
Proud of his men so devoted
His bid them a blessed adieu

His men with love and empathy wept
For their beloved general
Whose sorrow thrust into their heart
Their love of Lee welled full

Yea, through defeat the general
Still inspired such reverence
Nevermore had any such a claim as this
...or any ever since.

## Poet's Historical Notes:

Robert E. Lee was a West Point graduate serving in the Union Army until his resignation at the outbreak of the War Between the States, at which point he was appointed the commander of Virginia's military forces.[1] Lee proved to be an aggressive opponent and tactician, which brought the South many victories. He was a compassionate man whom was greatly loved and respected by his men.

General Lee became one of the best known and studied generals of history because of his profound foresight and mastery in war. The turning point in the war, the Battle of Gettysburg, changed the tide of victory towards the Union. General Robert E. Lee surrendered the Army of Northern Virginia to General Grant at the Appomatox Court House on April 9, 1865.[2] His surrender brought the long, bloody war closer to an end.

His victories still ring clear in the pages of history, brilliantly proving the South a fierce opponent in battle. Forever is his name linked with his beloved Virginia and the South, for which he sacrificed so much.

1 Henry, 35.

2 Alexander, 540.

# Jefferson Davis in Prison

Captors led the mocking
As prison walls upon him poured
Conspirators spoke the devil's word
Spreading lies to be well heard
Heard to keep the people talking
To keep alive the hateful flocking
To keep the nation riven in two
Stirring spite to heights anew.

Dank within those molded walls
Beyond the meager window barred
Paced the ever present guards
Ever watching their captive ward
Thumping incessant, hounding footfalls
Piercing the wound of pride it galls
Galling as his molding shoes
Galling as forbidding a fork to use
Enduring yet more bitter abuse.

Men came with shackles of iron one night
Davis roused with protest flaming
– against the outrage
– against the shaming
Fighting until they overcame
This man of age with biting chain.
Word of this degradation took flight
With the righteous pen of might
Pealing to hearts, this cruelty would wage
A protest to bind the nation in rage.

As written word spread the alarm
From reporting newspapers
Infuriating Southerners
Exasperating Northerners
Awaking public's forceful arm
Demanding the irons to be released
Northerners held the branch of peace
Aiding Davis with doctors and legal aid
Defending, befriending without pay
As his enemy now with outstretched hand
Gave the righteous boon of friend
Surely this was God's great plan
To bring war's bitterness to its end.

As Davis prayed God's will be done
Suffering years of imprisonment
– through the ailing
– through the failing
Whilst his fingers walking spent
Hours in Holy Testament
Awaiting justice for him to come
All the while praying "Thy will be done."

## Poet's Historical Notes:

Jefferson Davis was captured in May of 1865 and released in May of 1867.[1] His time in prison was a time of martyrdom. The injustice of his incarceration was blatant to most citizens, even in the North. During his imprisonment, his health deteriorated from the poor living conditions. Meanwhile, his wife and children were dealing with their own injustices.

Davis's wife, Varina is a prominent figure of the war as well. Her struggle and perseverance was extraordinary during and after the war. Varina and Jefferson were together with their children when he was captured. The traumatic effect this had on the children was a burden that she would have to bear alone. Furthermore, while Jefferson was in prison, she was held captive as well in Savannah, Georgia.[2] Forced to endure mocking and abuse, including the looting of her worldly goods left her and the children destitute.[3] When she finally gained her leave from Savannah, she actively crusaded for her husband's release.[4] Upon his release, he journeyed to be reunited with his adoring children whom he had missed for so long. Jefferson Davis peacefully lived the remainder of his years with his beloved Varina until his passing, in the winter of 1889.[5]

1 Cooper, 534, 564.
2 Davis, B., 206.
3 Davis, B., 146, 151, 206.
4 Davis, B., 215.
5 Cooper, 652-654.

# Thomas Stonewall Jackson

Thomas Stonewall Jackson, a military genius
Strictly self disciplined and intellectually focused
        Possessing incredible scope of imagination
        Mentally preparing for all possibilities
        Bold and daring with lightening decisiveness
        Shining with admirable dignity
Most beloved, this fearless leader
With blue eyes flashing in determination
        Flinching never from war's clamor
        Noble and steady facing battle's rigor
        With courage unfailing in gallant array
        Bidding devotion and bravery
        from his valiant men in Grey

A courteous and compassionate gentleman
Tenderly caring with empathy
    Modest and humble, loved by God
    Bearing impeccable integrity
    Inspiring example of Christian belief
    Deflecting his praise from victory
    – to God, he served, giving all glory
    Delighting in keeping His Holy Sabbath
        Studying God's precious Word, he loyally
        Found in It, serenity and peace
        Jackson, with a simple faith
        Lived the Word, in joy and grace

## Poet's Historical Notes:

Thomas "Stonewall" Jackson is a fascinating individual, whose life was cut short by the war. He possessed a numerous amount of peculiarities, which if one was not familiar with the man, would find him quite strange indeed. An example of one such oddity is his method of teaching. He taught at Virginia Military Institute before the War Between the States, and his mode of teaching was simply to lecture for the duration of the class. His lectures were prepared organized speeches from which he would not veer. This is quite boring, as one can imagine. Jackson was afflicted with an infirmity of the eyes, which made night reading forbidden, at the risk of blindness. Therefore, he read in the day that which he was to prepare for the following day's lesson, and then in the evening he would recall this information mentally, and analyzing it, he would prepare and organize the lecture for the next day, totally within his mind.[1]

There is much to say of the great Stonewall Jackson, but the most important is his faith. This truly is what made the man tick. Once he dedicated himself to God, he fervently sought and found an intimate relationship with his Maker. In that, he found peace. He believed that God loves all of His people equally, and in this, he too loved his fellow man, regardless of color. Jackson looked for slavery to end, but until that time he taught of a different freedom. He organized Sunday Schools for black people, and he taught them how to read and write, which was illegal.[2] In spite of the illegality of his actions, he pursued the scripture "Go therefore and make disciples of all nations" Matthew 28:19.

1 Dabney, 65.

2 Williams, 98.

# The Woolen Uniform

Poking through my cotton drawers
roasting in my uniform
itching like I got the bug
At my trousers I ashamedly tug
Reaching past my shoulder blade
scratching for releases aid
Embarrassed at this clown's charade
of dancing fumbling moves I made.
At last I shed the issued wear
Happily abandoning them without a care
Casting aside the coat and pants
my buddy questioned my lack of sense.
I told him "You can take the lot,
I've never been so miserably hot!"
He picked them up and put them on
Standing proudly in the uniform.
...His tattered cottons had bordered scandal
so his modesty was preserved – within my shamble.

Months went on as his stink fermented
making me believe he was truly demented
– wearing the woolen mass of string
turned my buddy to sulpher hot springs
My distance from him I carefully kept
as finally autumn relievedly crept
in to blot our sweat away
blessing us with cooler days.
Winter came most suddenly at night
covering us with snow by daylight.
...Cold...Wet...and Shivering...
My teeth and brain were clattering.
Through my cottons – feeling every stir
with every chill my agony endured.

Then dawning in my feeble mind
was the saving grace I had left behind
Now upon my buddy's form
keeping him, not me...Warm
I pleaded to his generosity
at last he smiled and gave to me
his cotton rags he had interchanged
when I had thought he was deranged.
I shiver less now than before
wishing I had kept that blamed uniform.

# The *Hunley*

Waiting for a crew of men
To take beneath the waves again
Trapping souls of courage within
Silence burying the crews thus far
the *Hunley*'s record, a bleeding scar.

Volunteers of brave, courageous men
Crowded the hull of the *Hunley* again
Training vigorously, by Lieutenant Dixon
Drilling on and off the shore
Ready for their chance at war.

Excitement in their quickened breast
Straining within Confederacies best
Orders revealed the *Hunley*'s quest
The mission: To sink a sloop of war
With the torpedo the *Hunley* bore.

Cruising the *Hunley* in darkened night
Beneath the water and out of sight
Suddenly a flurry of startled fright
Kindled the ship's crew that thought they spied
  A glimpse of something 'neath their starboard side.

Hastily, the torpedo struck the ship's belly
Reversing the *Hunley* in quickened fury
As the detonating cord from the torpedo pulled free
Exploding below the water line
    Erupting a gale into the sky.

The *Hunley* below the waters waited
Until the churning waters abated
Surfacing to signal the shore awaiting
The lantern of blue that Dixon was raising
    Seen through the fog, in victory praising.

Dixon, with his valiant men
The *Hunley* stole 'neath the waves again
Trapping the souls of courage within
As the *Hunley,* to the bottom cleaved
    Encompassing the crew, a watery grave received.

The first submarine to sink
A warship, opened history's link
To the mystery of why the *Hunley* sank
Too hard to raise, at that date
The *Hunley*'s salvage would have to wait.

A hundred years and more
Passed the *Hunley*'s crew before
Rescue came from their tomb of war
As their weary bones were free at last
To lay in earth, for their final rest.

Charleston, with her beauty gave
A funeral for the crew so brave
Hewing in her earth the graves
The streets were strewn with crowds to pay
Respect, and honor, to these men of the Grey.

## Poet's Historical Notes:

The CSS *Hunley* sank the USS *Housatonic* in Charleston Harbor in 1864; becoming the first submarine to sink an enemy ship successfully.[1] The extraordinary courage of the crews that manned the *Hunley* is remarkable. The first crew was courageous in undertaking the alien nature of submersion within this metal tube. The latter crews were courageous for becoming replacements for the crew that perished on the previous attempt.

The size of the *Hunley* was quite small and the men were very cramped. The overwhelming claustrophobia that would prohibit most people from such a feat is evident when seeing the exhibit in Charleston, or even diagrams and photos within both Edwin P. Hoyt's *The Voyage of the Hunley* and *Raising the Hunley* by Hicks and Kropf. The Charleston burial for Dixon and his crew honorably took place April 17, 2004.[2]

1 Hicks and Kropf, 2.

2 http://candlersonsofconfederacy.homestead.com/hunleyburialpage1.html

# No Man's Land

Silencing battle with shadowed wing
Night gazed o'er war's grisly scene
Spreading her cooling blanket of black
Easing the July swelter to slack

Sprinkling moonbeams from her hand
Across the bloodied Pennsylvania land
Bathing the gore with soft wisps of light
As moans gave sound to pair the sight

Beneath the cloak of twilight's shade
Mingled the Blue among the Grey
Gleaning from this bloody field
Comrades borne upon the shield

Piercing through the night's unrest
A voice in song for peace confessed
Alone he sang in tones so pure
Carrying home-sung hymns of yore

Reaching through the blinded night
Across the colours of wrong or right
Breaching hearts of every man
Cried the hymn from no man's land.

## Poet's Historical Notes:

As July 2, 1863 closed, the aftermath of the day's battle lay morbidly scattered across the Wheat Field. Hood's division had suffered miserably that day and the casualty rate was high. This was just one facet of the Battle of Gettysburg. In other areas, picket fire continually ensued over the regions of "no man's land." This account is so alluring because of the demonstrated compassion exhibited on both sides of the battlefield, which ceased their war for the night. The single voice that sang the church hymns lifted spirits weary of war and death, bringing that hope which comes with faith in Christ that was commonly shared by both the Grey and the Blue.

# The Ballad of Little Sorrel

Out of the stock cars he trod
To be chosen with a wink and a nod.

"For my wife this round Morgan will fare
His height to Anna, my wife finely pair."

A solid and muscular stallion he chose
A strong companion to war he supposed.

The end of the stallion's spotlight did near
When gunfire gave light the stallion's great fear.

The master turned to the Morgan he bought
Finding in him the traits that he sought.

He thought to himself the Morgan will do
Steady and calm with a heart ringing true.

The Morgan's intelligence and gate he prized
His first impression was wrong he surmised.

His decision made firm the Morgan he claimed
"Little Sorrel is what the steed's to be named."

Stonewall and Little Sorrel, to battle they flew
Trodding the battlegrounds of Grey and Blue.

Fearlessly carrying his master in war
Tiring never of the burden he bore.

Feeling the lurch of his master when hit
Little Sorrel clenched his mouth to the bit.

Stonewall loosed his grip from the rein
And fell from the Morgan in deathly pain.

The men carried Stonewall behind Confederate lines
As the Morgan saw his master for the last time.

Little Sorrel's brown eyes, gowned in sorrow
Shedding a tear, for no more tomorrow.

## Poet's Historical Notes:

Stonewall Jackson had chosen two horses with the intention being that the larger of the two would be his, and the smaller would be his wife's horse. The larger horse spooked with the noise of gunfire and had a rather uncomfortable gait. Thus, Jackson took another look at the smaller horse, a Morgan, and tried him out, finding the steed to be a perfect match for him. The mount, named Little Sorrel, had a nice easy gait, and was supremely reliable under battle fire, becoming a trusted companion for Stonewall. After Jackson died from his wounds, Little Sorrel was retired from the war.[1]

1 Williams, 172-173.

# DOCUMENTATION BY POEM

**The Ballad of Little Sorrel**
Williams, *Stonewall Jackson: The Black Man's Friend*, pp. 172-173.

**The Battle of the Crater**
Garrison, *Strange Battles of the Civil War*, pp. 260-268.
Commager, *The Blue and the Gray*, pp. 1018-1024.

**Belle Boyd**
Boyd, *Belle Boyd in Camp and in Prison*, pp. 6-7, 83-84, 87, 96-98, 103, 105-108 (under fire), 111, 118, 121, 131, 139, 161.
Sigaud, *Belle Boyd Confederate Spy*, pp. 25, 47-50, 93-95, 100, 127.

**The Bullet in the Book**
Davis, *The Orphan Brigade*, pp. 96.

**Colonel James Beard at the Battle of Mansfield**
Mitcham, *Richard Taylor and the Red River Campaign*, pp. 143, 157-158.
Winters, *The Civil War in Louisiana*, pp. 342.

**CSS *Virginia***
White, *The First Iron-Clad Naval Engagement in the World.*

**Doc Rayburn Meets Limber Jim**
**Doc Rayburn and his Phantom Unit**
http://www.rootsweb.ancestry.com/~arprairi/DocRay.htm
http://www.arkansasties.com/WhatsNew/2011/01/howell-a-doc-rayburn/

**Emma Sansom Meets General Forrest**
Davidson and Foxx, *Nathan Bedford Forrest*, pp. 143-149.
Henry, *The Story of the Confederacy*, pp. 291.

**The Escapades of Madame LaForte and Colonel Zarvona**
http://www.thelatinlibrary.com/chron/civilwarnotes/zarvona.html

**Freedom's Fight**
Dabney, *Life and Campaigns of Lieut. Gen. Thomas J. Jackson*, pp. 125-176.
Henry, *The Story of the Confederacy*, pp. 13-15, 34-35, 471.

**General Lewis Addison Armistead**
Stewart, *Pickett's Charge*, pp. 180, 216-219.
Commager, *The Blue and the Gray*, pp. 628-630.

**The *Hunley***
Hicks and Kropf, *Raising the Hunley*, pp.44-65, 70-75, 77, 83-84.
Hoyt, *The Voyage of the Hunley*, pp. 24, 43-75, 78, 109, 115.
The date of Dixon crew's burial is from the website:
http://candlersonsofconfederacy.homestead.com/hunleyburialpage1.html

**J.E.B. Stuart's Raid on General Pope**
Dabney, *Life and Campaigns of Lieut. Gen. Thomas J. Jackson*, pp. 514-515.
McClellan, *I Rode With Jeb Stuart*, pp. 94-95.

**Jefferson Davis**
Cooper, *Jefferson Davis, American*, pp. 3-8, 15-17, 20, 21, 23, 29, 40, 85-86, 88, 98-99, 102, 106-107, 164, 327-329, 548-549, 552-553, 635, 658.
Davis, B. *The Long Surrender*, pp. 178, 201, 223.

**Jefferson Davis in Prison**
Cooper, *Jefferson Davis, American*, pp. 534, 548, 549, 554, 564, 652-654.
Davis, B. *The Long Surrender*, pp. 144-146, 151, 173, 178, 179, 181-182, 204-207, 215, 218, 222-223.

**Joanna Fox Waddill**
http://www.lib.lsu.edu/special/findaid/w4578.html

**John S. Mosby Captures General Stoughton**
Mosby, *Memoirs of Colonel John S. Mosby*, pp. 172-182.
Wert, *Mosby's Rangers*, pp. 18-22; promotion to colonel, pp. 264.

**Matthew Fontaine Maury**
Hearn, *Tracks of the Sea*, pp. 6, 23, 63-66, 81, 92-94, 102, 113-114, 121, 124, 174, 178-179.
Corbin, *A Life of Matthew Fontaine Maury*, pp. 8, 16-23, 158-160, 199-203, 215.
Maury, R. L., *A Brief Sketch of the Work of Matthew Fontaine Maury*, pp. 4-5, 16, 30-31.
Maury, *The Physical Geography of the Sea*, pp. 87, 103, 241, 283.

**The Men of Pickett's Charge**
Stewart, *Pickett's Charge*, pp. 139-140, 149-150, 169-170, 180, 209-270.

**Nancy Hart**
http://www.nkclifton.com/nancy.html Accessed 2013.
http://www.nkclifton.com/nancyh.shoots.html Accessed 2013.

**No Man's Land**
Wilkinson and Woodworth, *A Scythe of Fire*, pp. 253-254.

**The Orphan Brigade**
Davis, *The Orphan Brigade*, pp. 10-12 (loyalties), 13 (confederate camp), 16 (Kentucky 1st born), 24-25 (confederate troops banished from Kentucky), 27 (spirit), 85-97 (battle), 99-100, 128-129 (character), 130 (Orphan's status), 131 (conduct), 135 (Kentucky lost to Union), 136 (spirit), 138 (mail), 144-145 (battle), 147 (Bragg's spite), 152-161 (Murfreesboro), 176 (rear guard), 180-192, 198-200, 201-202 (homesick), 204 (spirit), 217-236, 240, 245 (spirit), 250-251, 257.
Brown, *The Civil War in Kentucky*, pp. 271, 273 (finest soldiers), 276-277, 280, 284-290.

**Patrick Cleburne at Ringgold Gap**
Symonds, *Stonewall of the West*, pp. 171-177.
___, *A Meteor Shining Brightly*, pp. 114-139.
___, *The Civil War in Kentucky*, pp. 238.

**The Picket's Truce**
Davis, *The Orphan Brigade*, pp. 220.
Wilkinson and Woodworth, *A Scythe of Fire*, pp. 111.

**Raphael Semmes and the *Alabama***
Fox, *Wolf of the Deep*, pp. 7, 52, 53, 55, 59 (Pirate of the Seas), 62-63, 68, 76 (mutiny), 82, 86, 88, 98, 99, 126-127, 149, 158-159, 171-174, 179 (mutiny), 183-184, 198, 207-208, 210-213 (Cherbourg), 219-228 (Kearsarge), 233, 236, 237 (promotion).
Henry, *The Story of the Confederacy*, pp. 234-235, 407.

**Robert E. Lee**
Maurice, *Robert E. Lee: The Soldier*, pp. 292-294.
Alexander, *Fighting for the Confederacy*, pp.539-540.

**Thomas Stonewall Jackson**
Dabney, *Life and Campaigns of Lieutenant General T.J. (Stonewall) Jackson*, 18, 36, 46, 48-50, 52, 65, 67, 71, 74-75, 78, 79, 85-92, 95, 98-100, 103 (prayer), 105, 109, 189, 191-195, 197-198, 202-203, 205, 212, 220-229(First Manassas), 248-249, 261-270, 285, 313-322 (battle), 350, 360-383 (battle), 388, 404-430(battle), 439, 444-456 (battle), 470, 484-485, 490 (Glory), 492-503 (battle), 516-538 (battle), 540-541, 553-555, 563, 565, 578-579, 587-588 (faith), 589, 592, 595-598 (battle), 608-622 (battle), 628, 640-643 (faith), 656, 661-667 (battle planning), 670-686 (battle), 706-710, 719, 722-723 (faith), 733-740.
Williams, *Stonewall Jackson: The Black Man's Friend*, pp. 50-51, 54, 98, 102-103, 115, 126, 139.

**Turner Ashby**
Dabney, *Life and Campaigns of Lieut. Gen. Thomas J. Jackson*, pp. 260-261, 327, 396-403.

# BIBLIOGRAPHY

Alexander, General Edward Porter. *Fighting for the Confederacy.* Edited by Gary W. Gallagher. Chapel Hill, NC: University of North Carolina Press, 1989.

Boyd, Belle. *Belle Boyd in Camp and Prison.* Baton Rouge: Louisiana State University Press, 1998.

Brown, Kent Masterson, editor. *The Civil War in Kentucky: Battle For the Bluegrass State.* Mason City, IA: Savas Publishing Company, 2000.

Commager, Henry Steele. *The Blue and The Gray.* New York: Fairfax Press, 1982.

Cooper, William, Jr. *Jefferson Davis, American.* New York: Alfred A. Knopf, 2000.

Corbin, Diana Fontaine. *A Life of Matthew Fontaine Maury.*

Dabney, R. L. *Life and Campaigns of Lieut. Gen. Thomas J. Jackson.* Harrisonburg, VA: Sprinkle Publications, 1983.

Davidson, Eddy W., and Foxx, Daniel. *Nathan Bedford Forrest: In Search of the Enigma.* Gretna, LA: Pelican Publishing Company, 2007.

Davis, Burke. *The Long Surrender.* New York: Vintage Books, 1989.

Davis, William C. *The Orphan Brigade: The Kentucky Confederates Who Couldn't Go Home.* Baton Rouge: Louisiana State University Press, 1983.

Fox, Stephen. *Wolf of the Deep: Raphael Semmes and the Notorious Confederate Raider CSS Alabama.* New York: Alfred A. Knopf, 2007.

Garrison, Webb, Jr. *Strange Battles of the Civil War.* Nashville: Cumberland House, 2001.

Hearn, Chester G. *Tracks in the Sea: Matthew Fontaine Maury and the Mapping of the Oceans.* Crawfordsville, IN: International Marine, 2002.

Henry, Robert Selph. *The Story of the Confederacy.* Revised Edition. Old Saybrook, CT: Konecky & Konecky, 1999.

Hicks, Brian and Kropf, Schuyler. *Raising the Hunley.* New York: Ballantine Books, 2002.

Hoyt, Edwin P. *The Voyage of the Hunley.* Short Hills, NJ: Burford Books, 2002.

Joslyn, Mauriel Phillips, editor. *A Meteor Shining Brightly: Essays on Maj. Gen. Patrick R. Cleburne.* Milledgeville, GA: Terrell House Publishing, 1999.

Maurice, Frederick. *Robert E. Lee: The Soldier.* New York: Bonanza Books, 1925.

Maury, Matthew Fontaine. *The Physical Geography of the Sea.* Edited by John Leighly. Reprint Edition. Mineola, NY: Dover Publications, 2003.

Maury, Richard, L. *A Brief Sketch of the Work of Matthew Fontaine Maury During the War, 1861-1865.* Richmond: Whittet & Shepperson, 1915.

McClellan, Henry, B. *I Rode With Jeb Stuart: The Life and Campaigns of Major General J.E.B. Stuart.* Reprint Edition. New York: Da Capo Press, 1994.

Mosby, John S. *Memoirs of Colonel John S. Mosby.* Edited by Charles Wells Russell. Reprint Edition. Millwood, NY: Kraus Reprint, 1990.

Mitcham, Samuel W., Jr. *Richard Taylor and the Red River Campaign of 1864.* Gretna, LA: Pelican Publishing Company, 2012.

NKJV: Scripture taken from the New King James Version. ©1982 by Thomas Nelson, Inc. Used by permission. All rights reserved.

Sigaud, Louis A. *Belle Boyd Confederate Spy.* Richmond: The Dietz Press, Inc., 1944.

Sorrel, General G. Moxley. *At the Right Hand of Longstreet.* Reprint Edition. Lincoln, NE: University of Nebraska Press, Bison Books Edition, 1999.

Stewart, George. *Pickett's Charge: A Microhistory of the Final Attack at Gettysburg, July 3, 1863.* Boston: Houghton Mifflin Company, 1987.

Symonds, Craig L. *Stonewall of the West: Patrick Cleburne and the Civil War.* Lawrence, KS: University Press of Kansas, 1997.

Wert, Jeffry D. *Mosby's Rangers.* New York: Simon and Schuster, 1990.

White, E. V. *The First Iron-Clad Naval Engagement in the World: History of the Facts of the Great Naval Battle.* New York: J. S. Ogilvie Publishing Company, 1906.

Wilkinson, Warren and Woodworth, Steven E. *A Scythe of Fire: A Civil War Story of the Eighth Georgia Infantry Regiment.* New York: William Morrow, 2002.

Williams, Richard G. *Stonewall Jackson: The Black Man's Friend.* Nashville: Cumberland House Publishing, 2006.

Winters, John D. *The Civil War in Louisiana.* Baton Rouge: Louisiana State University Press, 1991.

# INTERNET REFERENCES

http://candlersonsofconfederacy.homestead.com/hunleyburialpage1.html. Accessed 2013.

The Latin Library. Richard Thomas Zarvona (1833-1875). Accessed 2012 from http://www.thelatinlibrary.com/chron/civilwarnotes/zarvona.html.

Library of Louisiana State University, 1997. Waddill Family Papers. Accessed 2012 from http://www.lib.lsu.edu/special/findaid/w4578.html.

http://www.arkansasties.com/WhatsNew/2011/01/howell-a-doc-rayburn/. Accessed 2013.

http://www.nkclifton.com/nancy.html. Accessed 2013.

http://www.nkclifton.com/nancyh.shoots.html. Accessed 2013.

http://www.rootsweb.ancestry.com/~arprairi/DocRay.htm. Accessed 2013.

# About the Author

Zelma Kay Halemeyer resides in rural Golden Eagle, Illinois, where her paternal family has lived for four generations. In the peaceful atmosphere that is her home, she treasures God's every day wonders, from which she finds joy and inspiration.

Zelma's maternal family is steeped with a rich history of Confederate heritage. Her Southern ancestry drove her to read accounts of Confederate history, thus inspiring a sympathy for the often misunderstood Confederacy. Through her research, she was moved to write her vision of Confederate history. Thus, her first book was completed, *Rebel Grey: Poems of Confederate History.*

Zelma graduated with honors from Southern Illinois University at Carbondale, Illinois, where she earned a Bachelor of Arts degree in Music. She has always had a strong interest in the arts and is an avid reader of history.